T0387751

OOPS! ACCIDENTAL INVENTIONS

ICE CREAM CONES

by Catherine C. Finan

Consultant: Beth Gambro
Reading Specialist, Yorkville, Illinois

Minneapolis, Minnesota

Teaching Tips

Before Reading

- Look at the cover of the book. Discuss the picture and the title.

- Ask readers to brainstorm a list of what they already know about ice cream cones. What can they expect to see in this book?

- Go on a picture walk, looking through the pictures to discuss vocabulary and make predictions about the text.

During Reading

- Read for purpose. Encourage readers to think about ice cream cones as they are reading.

- Ask readers to look for the details of the book. What happened to take the ice cream cone from an accident to a favorite treat?

- If readers encounter an unknown word, ask them to look at the sounds in the word. Then, ask them to look at the rest of the page. Are there any clues to help them understand?

After Reading

- Encourage readers to pick a buddy and reread the book together.

- Ask readers to name two things that happened when the ice cream cone was being developed. Find the pages that tell about these things.

- Ask readers to write or draw something they learned about ice cream cones.

Credits:
Cover and title page, © karandaev/iStock; 3, © StockImageFactory.com/Shutterstock; 5, © wundervisuals/iStock; 7, © stephanie phillips/iStock; 9, © ClassicStock/Alamy; 10, © Puripat1981/iStock; 11, © sanleer/iStock; 12–13, © Randy Duchaine/Alamy; 14–15, © igmarx/iStock; 16–17, © Sueddeutsche Zeitung Photo/Alamy; 19, © GracePhotos/Shutterstock; 20–21, © ahirao_photo/iStock; 22TL, © JulPo/iStock; 22TR, © Swanya Charoonwatana/iStock; 22BM, © AaronAmat/iStock; 23BM, © RiverNorthPhotography/iStock; 23TL, © StockRocket/iStock; 23TR, © Philip Scalia/Alamy; and 23BL, © rjp85/iStock; 23BR.

Library of Congress Cataloging-in-Publication Data

Names: Finan, Catherine C., 1972- author.
Title: Ice cream cones / by Catherine C. Finan.
Description: Minneapolis : Bearport Publishing, [2023] | Series: Bearcub
books. Oops! accidental inventions | Includes bibliographical references
and index.
Identifiers: LCCN 2022034225 (print) | LCCN 2022034226 (ebook) | ISBN
9798885093439 (library binding) | ISBN 9798885094658 (paperback) | ISBN
9798885095808 (ebook)
Subjects: LCSH: Ice cream cones--History--Juvenile literature.
Classification: LCC TX795 .F44 2023 (print) | LCC TX795 (ebook) | DDC
641.86--dc23/eng/20220721
LC record available at https://lccn.loc.gov/2022034225
LC ebook record available at https://lccn.loc.gov/2022034226

Copyright © 2023 Bearport Publishing Company. All rights reserved. No part of this publication may be reproduced in whole or in part, stored in any retrieval system, or transmitted in any form or by any means, electronic, mechanical, photocopying, recording, or otherwise, without written permission from the publisher.

For more information, write to Bearport Publishing, 5357 Penn Avenue South, Minneapolis, MN 55419.

Contents

A Tasty Accident 4

Ice Cream Cones Today 22

Glossary 23

Index 24

Read More 24

Learn More Online 24

About the Author 24

A Tasty Accident

It is fun to eat ice cream from a cone.

Yum!

How did this tasty **invention** happen?

The first ice cream cones were made in the 1890s.

They helped fix a problem.

What happened?

It all started in New York.

A man named Italo sold ice cream there.

He served the snack in glass cups.

Sometimes, Italo ran out of cups.

Oops!

He could not sell ice cream without them.

Then, Italo had an idea.

He made a cup out of a **waffle**.

It was the first ice cream cone!

People wanted more cones.

So, Italo built a **machine.**

It made many waffle cones quickly!

A few years later, there was a big **fair** in Missouri.

Someone made ice cream cones there, too.

Even more people tried the treat.

Over time, people made new ice cream cones.

Some were dipped in things.

Do you like cones with chocolate and sprinkles?

Today, there are many kinds of ice cream cones.

People still love this tasty treat!

Ice Cream Cones Today

How much ice cream can go in a cone? The **record** is 125 scoops!

One company makes more than 2 billion cones each year.

The biggest ice cream cone ever was taller than a Christmas tree!

Glossary

fair a big event where many things are shown and sold

invention something new that people have made

machine a thing with parts that work together to do something

record the most something has ever been

waffle a kind of thin, flat cake

Index

chocolate 18, 22
fair 16
machine 14
Missouri 16
New York 8
waffle 12, 14

Read More

Miller, Derek. *Ice Cream (The Making of Everyday Things).* New York: Cavendish Square, 2020.

Neuenfeldt, Elizabeth. *Milk to Ice Cream (Blastoff! Readers: Beginning to End).* Minneapolis: Bellwether Media, 2021.

Learn More Online

1. Go to **www.factsurfer.com** or scan the QR code below.
2. Enter **"Ice Cream Cones"** into the search box.
3. Click on the cover of this book to see a list of websites.

About the Author

Catherine C. Finan is a writer living in northeast Pennsylvania. During the summer, her favorite lunch is a big ice cream cone!